A SOUL DEFINED

MIRANDA LEIGH

To the beautiful people in my life known as my family and friends....
I see you, I hear you, I love you, and I thank you. I'm so grateful for the time we have shared and the time we will share. You bring me joy and inspire me in so many ways.

To my amazing husband and daughter....
You make me incredibly happy every day. Thank you for being you and always encouraging me to face my fears and achieve my goals. I love you always.

Repeat

Has it all been done before
Has it all been said before
Stuck in a pattern
Rewind, repeat
Rewind, repeat
The same song
The same verse
Once more
Don't ignore
The urge to change
The station
Change the channel

The Weight

Maybe I don't want to feel
The weight of your pain
On my shoulders
The weight of your worries
Crushing my bones
Maybe I don't want the stain
On my soul
Maybe I want a clean slate
Before it's too late
Maybe it's taken it's toll

Surrender

When the dust settles
When the winds
Die down
When the tide subsides
Can you surrender
To the calm
Or will you
Create another storm

Consumption

Why do we insist
On over indulgence
Why do we insist
On gluttonous consumption
Why can't we refrain
When we know the result
Will be the same

Apologize

Why do we apologize
For what we want
What we don't want
Who we are
Who we are not

Weightless

I am the paper
You are the paper weight
I just want to float off the desk
Make a mess on the floor
But there you are
Holding me firmly in place

Circles

I think I've been moving forward
I think I've been moving backward
Maybe I've lost
My sense of direction
Maybe I've found it
I think I've been walking
In a circle
Somehow ending
At the beginning

Sugar

The rapid movement
The familiar gleam
In the eye
Temporarily satisfied
Craving subsides
Yet lingers
Never disappears
Should I be concerned
Will you ever learn
To take control
Or will you always
Want more , take more
Let it devour
You whole

Full Bloom

In full bloom
Need to consume
No more room
Better resume
In full bloom

The Busy

How easy it is
To lose sight
Of yourself
Caught up In the busy
Caught up in the life
Some times you just have
To stop
To remember
To recognize

Dig

Can you dig a little deeper
Get to the bottom of it
Uncover the root
Beneath the earth
Can you dig a little more
Identify the nature
Of the source

Go

Follow me
Lead me
Guide me
Where do we want to go
What do we want to know
Where do we want to be
What do we want to see

The Key

I've lost the key
Can't unlock the mystery
I've lost my mind
Can't finish the rhyme
Maybe if I keep looking
Maybe if I follow the signs
I'll find it in time

Confront

No more running
No more hiding
It's time to seek
Confrontation
It's time to find out
What fills up the space
It's time to let go
Of what has been confined
Within your skin
Within your soul

Pieces

We are really all the same
We are really all alike
We are really all just pieces
Trying to fit
Into the puzzle of life

Stand Out

Don't fade into the background
Don't blend into the crowd
Don't follow
Don't wilt, don't shrink
Forget how to think
Find your voice
Make a choice
Shine bright
Stand out
Let your colors shout
Find your pride
Stand tall
Step out of the shadows
And into the light

Climb

How quickly we can transport
Ourselves back in time
Flooded by memories
How do we fight
Against the current
Climb back into the now

Gaze

Can you set your gaze
Move with intention
Step by step, day by day
Toward your vision

In the Clouds

Head in the clouds
Words whispered by the breeze
Head in the clouds
High above the trees
Head in the clouds
Drifting in peace
Head in the clouds
Dreaming of the sea

Heat

Feel the internal heat rise
Blood boiling beneath the skin
Don't let it simmer
Let it vent through your pores
Vaporize before your eyes

Scrambled

Stuck within four walls
Can't seem to turn the water off
Can't stop the rain
Words dripping inside my brain
Hard to focus
Watch the time crawl by
Words begin to scramble
A tangled knot
waiting to be untied

Torn

A soul divided
Simply torn in two
One side aches with the old
One side celebrates with the new

Guilt

There you are
Sitting on my shoulder
A burden to carry
A shadow lurking
In the corner of my mind
Always wanting sacrifice
Always wanting compromise
Wish you would fall away
Leave me be
Free to enjoy it all

Procrastination

Are you treading
In the waters of procrastination
Swimming in a sea of excuses
What are you waiting for
The time is now
You are ready

Destination

When your dream
And your reality
Become one
Your song will tell the story
Of your journey
Your painting will reveal
The colors of your destination

Pop the Cork

I see you
A bottle
Full of emotions
Filled to the brink
Should probably
Pop the cork
Let the words
Spill into the glass
Avoid an explosion

Buzz

Can you feel the power
Can you hear the buzz
Of your energy
Listen to its directions
Find the synergy

Navigate

I must've fallen asleep
At the wheel
Somehow
I'm awake now
Standing at the helm
Ready to navigate
The sails

Slow Burn

Can you feel the slow burn
Of your essence
Simmering beneath your core
Too bright to ignore
Fan the flames
Nurture the coals
Feel it grow
Inside your soul

Gravity

Can you feel
The pull
Of gravity
Will you go
With the flow
Or stay
Out of the way

Life Explodes

Beads of sweat glisten
Like drops of dew
On your skin
Breath ignites
Light to heavy
Pulse quickens
Life explodes
Within you
Begging you to listen

Growing

Think I'm emerging
Out of my shell
Think I'll leave it empty
On the side of the road
Safely behind me

Connection

Can you be present
In your mind
Present in your body
Feel the connection
The soul within the skin
Can you be in tune
To the rhythm
Of your breath
In tune to the
moment in time

Let Go

So hard to let go
Of what you know
The old familiar road
Worn and traveled
So hard to let go
Of the fears
You've held onto for years
Be brave
In the face
Of the unknown

On the Surface

So many words
We've exchanged
So many words
Scattered on the surface
Skin deep
In shallow waters
Revealing nothing
That matters

Time

You can't solve
Every problem
You can't fix it all
Sometimes you have
To let them fall
Let them be broken
Make the wrong choice
Be the wrong person
You have to let them heal
Let them feel how they feel
Let them fail
Let them grow
Let them learn
Sometimes you have to let go
Let time work it's magic
Let time fix it all

Poetry

Poetry is everywhere
It exists all around us
In the beauty of nature
The magic of the stars
The rhythm of the rain
The rhyme of the tides
The warmth of sunshine
The chill of a breeze
The words spoken
The love shared
The lyrics of a song
The motion of a dance
The mystery of life

Impulse

Scratch the itch
Cave to the craving
Fulfill the desire
Grant the wish
Of the impulse

Butterflies

Stomach drops to the knees
A knot full of anxieties
Butterflies impatiently
Awaiting their release

Adolescence

Adolescence
The wild ride
Of the internal
Roller coaster
Highs
Lows
Everything
Nothing
Craziness
Laziness
Lust
Disgust
Guilt
Innocence
Out of control
The wild ride
Of the internal
Roller coaster
Of adolescence

Crackle of Life

Crackle of fire
Warmth of laughter
Stories told
Never grow old
Memories mold
Together we hold
Warmth of love
Crackle of life

The Journey

The journey
Has only just begun
Still have miles to run
Beneath the sun
Beneath the moon
Beneath the stars
Miles and miles
Dusk to dawn
On and on

What Defines You

The chase
The race
The search
The game
Powerful
Powerless
Go the distance
What is waiting
At the finish line
Will you see
Will you find
Will you be
What defines you

Break

Break through
Break out
Break down
Break free

Rhythm

Feel the rhythm
Of your breath
The rise and fall
Connect
To the rhythm
Of your life
Surrender
To all that lies
Within your skin

Doubt

The hesitation
The pause
The space
Creates a hole
For doubt to fill
An invitation
For excuses

Waves of Today

Don't be swallowed
By the seas of yesterday
Don't wait for
The tides of tomorrow
Dive into the surf
Ride the waves of today

Spirits

Drinks flow
The buzz grows
Spirits lift
Laughter drifts
Music flies
Hours dance by
Before you realize
It's time to go
Time to face
The promise of tomorrow

Cloud

A cloud of sadness
Hovers overhead
Lingering. Threatening
To drizzle
To pour
To soak
You to the core

Control

Are we
The writers
Or our story
The creators
Of our destiny
Do we have control
Are we lost
In our own journey
Drowning in our own sea

Bare

Old lungs
Breathe
Stale air
Old bones
Grow brittle
Old souls
Grow bare
Beauty lingers
There

Keep Going

Don't leave me behind
Don't let me rewind
Don't let me wallow
Don't leave me hollow
Keep moving, keep going
I'll find a way to follow
Keep moving, keep going
I'll find a way to grow

Do We?

Do we have to be lost
In order to be found
Do we have to create sound
In order to hear silence
Do we have to feel broken
In order to feel whole
Do we have to see
Where we are going
In order to know
Where we are

Thread

Lost in space
Running in place
Time travels
Stillness unravels
Thoughts race
Inside your head
Hanging by a thread

The Sun

What if the sun
Was to shine
All through the night
What if the sun
Was always in sight
The brightest star
The brightest light
Would we miss the darkness
Or would it be all right

We are More

We are more
Than our choices
We are more
Than our mistakes
We are more
Than our voices
We are more
Than pretty faces
We are more
Than mortal bodies
Taking up space
We are more

Waste

Don't waste your time
Don't waste your energy
Don't bother to fall apart
It's only temporary
It doesn't deserve your worry
It can't change your heart

Champagne

The bubbles rise
The light shimmers
The bubbles fizz
The light glimmers
The bubbles settle
The light dims
Can you feel the glow
Can you taste the sparkle

Absence

Your absence
Is present
In the quiet
In the empty
In the hollow ache
Your presence
Is absent
In my sleep
In my wake
In my bones
In my soul

Night

The face
Of the moon
The patten
If the stars
The darkness
Of the sky
The breath
Of night
Swallowed by
The light

Satisfy

What will satisfy
Your hunger
What will quench
Your thirst
What will fulfill
Your desire
What will ignite
Your fire

Ready

Are you inspired
Because you're happy
Are you happy
Because you're inspired
Are you ready
Because you're free
Are you free
Because you're ready

Power

Power
Where does it reside
Where does it lie
Is it buried deep inside
Don't let it hide
Turn on the light
Find it
Let it radiate
Illuminate
Be powerful

Yoga

Yoga
Show up
Open the door
To your mind
Your body will follow
Find your expression
Reveal your truth
Your unique light
Wrapped in skin

Explosion

Maybe it's time
To let the words fly
Maybe it's time
For the tears to fall
Maybe it's worth the explosion
To avoid the erosion

Evolve

Confined within
The walls of conflict
Smothered by
The flames of rage
Frozen, paralyzed by fear
Climb the walls
Extinguish the flames
Break the ice
Face it, fight
Conquer
Resolve to evolve

Beneath the surface

Exposed
In a place
Of reflection
Open your eyes
Make the connection
Look beyond the image
See beneath the surface

Restless

Restless winds stir
Restless souls whisper
Restless minds wonder
Restless bodies wander
Restless winds blow
Restless souls know
Restless minds search
Restless bodies lurch

Intersections

All the paths connect
Intersections of change
Unavoidable , inevitable
Choose a direction
Don't look for perfection

Listen

Close your eyes
Listen
To the leaves fall
Listen
To the moon rise
Listen
To the darkness spread
Listen
To the stars arrive
Listen
To the quiet
Close your eyes

Go

Believe
Achieve
Know
Go

A Sea

Imagine a sea
Of endless possibility
Imagine a sea
Of infinite beauty
Of radiant colors , radiant life
Waiting to be discovered
Imagine a sea
Full of mysteries
Waiting to be solved

Release

I'll take you there
To the edge
To the brink
To the limit
To the end
I'll release you there
Set you free

Intuition

Intuition
The light of instinct
The echo
Of your inner voice
Leading you
Guiding you
If you choose
To listen
Intuition

Winter's Song

Warmth of fire light
Trees shiver in the night
Snow flakes dance along
To winters song
Chilled to the bone
And all alone
Warmth of fire light

Breath of Winter

Icy breath of winter
Fills your lungs
Escapes your lips
A cloud of misery
Icy breath of winter
Chills your flesh
To the bone
Toes to finger tips
Forcing them to shiver
Icy breath of winter
Covers the earth in frost
So much beauty lost

Radiate

Do what makes you happy
Do what sets you free
Allows you to transcend
To radiate, to be content

Refresh

Breath is alive
With the rhythm
Of the tides
Let it rise through you
Let it wash over you
Refresh your life

Alive in the Moment

Numb with nerves
Blank with fear
Frozen in anticipation
Quivering in your skin
Breathe in courage
Breathe in confidence
Feel Alive in the moment
You deserve

Vision

It's all happening
It's all coming together
A blurred vision
Brought into focus
A mission accomplished
A dream brought to life
An end
Unites
With a
Beginning

Like the Tree

It's okay to be
Like the tree
To reach for the sky
To let go
Of pieces of yourself
Let them fall away
Leaves floating
It's okay to rise
From your buried roots
To grow beyond your height
It's okay to be
Like the tree

Freedom Lives

Freedom lives
In the breath of the trees
The falling leaves
The break of the ocean
The wake of the sunrise
Freedom lives
In the breath of a soul
The falling tears
The break of a heart
A smile that wakes the eyes
Freedom lives

Surprise

Memories fleeting
Shallow breathing
Rapid beating
Eager eyes
Taken by surprise

Listless

Listlessly meandering
Wistfully winding
Back in time
Stuck in a maze
Blocked by scar tissue
Keep going , keep working
Find your way back
To your smile , to the now

Road of Love

The love between us
Stretches on and on
A road with bumps and turns
That leads to everywhere
And always back again

Eternity

The faucet of time
Floods your life so fast
You struggle to catch your breath
Or it trickles
Drip by Drip
Second by second
Into the bucket of eternity

Firework

The match has been lit
The spark ignited
Watch as the sparkles fly
Into the sky
To greet the stars
Explode in shades of rainbows
Falling before your eyes

Gratitude

Don't forget
Gratitude
Don't forget
To appreciate
All that you are
All that you know
All the little things
The universe
Has to offer

Crave

What do you crave
A warm embrace
A quiet space
The sun on your face
The feel of crashing waves
The sound of soft rain
The smell of fall
The taste of snow flakes
What do you crave

Gather

Gather
Celebrate love
Appreciate togetherness
Be present
Cherish the moments
That create the memories
That linger in your mind
That warm your soul
That last a lifetime

Follows

Create movement
Stillness follows
Let yourself fall
Then rise above
Be broken
Strength follows
Ask questions
Then find the answers

Flourish

Kindness
Compassion
Love
Gratitude
Freedom to be
Who you are
These are the things
That matter always
Let them be the roots
From which you flourish

Tradition

A special repetition
Carved in stone
Carved in time
Some old, some new
A special celebration
Carved in stone
Carved in time
Created to be continued
Tradition

Love for Days

Been thinking for hours
The words circling
Inside my heart, inside my brain
Trying to find their way
To express how much it means
That you have loved me
For so many days
That you have loved me
In so many ways
I guess I'll just say
I know I'll love you
For all of my days
I know I'll love you
In all of the ways

Transformation

See the beauty
See the light
Watch it unfold
Watch it ignite
Let it be a revelation
Let it be an inspiration
Amuse, Amaze
Hold your gaze
A transformation

Intensify

Electrify .
Magnify.
Intensify.
Don't deny
Don't defy
What's inside

Meditation

Everyone should pause
Take the time to meditate
To melt into a space
Transcend to a happy place
Close your eyes
Paint the details
On the walls of your mind
You will find
A peaceful escape
A blissful state
Surrender to the zen
And know
You can always
Come back again

Embrace

Approach
When they seem
Unapproachable
Reach
When they seem
Unreachable
Pull them in
Embrace them
With your strength
Embrace them
With your love
Hold them closer
When they want to let go
They need you
More than you know

A Day

One of those days
Nothing goes your way
Everything is lost
Nothing good to say
It will be okay
Tomorrow is a new day
Everything goes your way
All is found
Only good things to say
All is okay

Slow

Go slow
Feel every breath
Go slow
Listen to every word
Go slow
Soak in the moment
Go slow
Absorb the glow

Euphoric Atmosphere

Music plays
In the background
Lyrics fill the void
Move to the rhythm
Let the lyrics linger
Let them resonate
Let them create
The vibration
A euphoric atmosphere

Lines

So many lines
Drawn in the sand
In between
Above
Below
So many lines
to follow
To land between
Above
Below
So many lines
To cross
To avoid
To draw
To erase
In the sand

Memories

So many memories
Created In a lifetime
Some leave bruises
Hide deep inside
Some rise to the surface
Fill you to the brink with joy
Some leave you
With the taste
Of bittersweet nostalgia
Lingering
On the tip of your tongue
Settling at the bottom
Of your soul

Soulmate

Do you hear
What I hear
Do you see
What I see
Do you feel
What I feel
When your soul
Speaks to mine
When my soul
Speaks to yours

A Note

Today
I found a note
To end on
Tomorrow
I hope to find
A note
To begin upon

About the Author

I am the author of A Soul Adrift, a massage therapist and yoga instructor . I have been writing poetry since I was 17. My passions include poetry, yoga, family, music, sunshine, the ocean, and life in general. I have a loving husband and daughter that inspire me every day. I am an optimist who believes in the power of positivity .

Made in the USA
Coppell, TX
02 July 2020